Lean Startup: Key to a Better Chance of Successful Startup

By Ade Asefeso MCIPS MBA

Second Edition

ISBN-13: 978-1499774580

ISBN-10: 1499774583

Publisher: AA Global Sourcing Ltd
Website: http://www.aaglobalsourcing.com

Table of Contents

Disclaimer...5

Dedication..6

Chapter 1: Lean Startup Business Ideas 7

Chapter 2: Knowing What it Takes.........................11

Chapter 3: Even Before the Beginning...................13

Chapter 4: Research the Market 19

Chapter 5: Business Start-up Legal Requirements 25

Chapter 6: Business Plan.......................................29

Chapter 7: Essential Elements of a Good Business Plan..33

Chapter 8: The Devil is in the Details 35

Chapter 9: Managing Finance 41

Chapter 10: Tips on Financial Planning 43

Chapter 11: Lets Go on a Treasure Hunt 47

Chapter 12: Hiring Tips for Lean Startup 53

Chapter 13: The Way forward................................61

Chapter 14: Keep it Lean.......................................69

Chapter 15: Lean Startup Deployment...................73

Chapter 16: Additional Lean Startup Concepts 77

Chapter 17: Create Pre-Launch Demand...............79

Chapter 18: Deploy Decision like a Lean Startup.83

Chapter 19: Think Big, Start Small.........................91

Chapter 20: The Promise of the Lean Startup 93

Chapter 21: A Lean Startup Doesn't Necessarily Mean Small..99

Chapter 22: Top 10 Ways Entrepreneurs Pivot a Lean Startup...103
Chapter 23: Some Criticism of Lean Startup.......107
Chapter 24: Managing Change and Growth in Startup...111
Chapter 25: Conclusion 117
Resource and References...121

Disclaimer

This publication is designed to provide competent and reliable information regarding the subject matter covered. However, it is sold with the understanding that the author and publisher are not engaged in rendering professional advice. The authors and publishers specifically disclaim any liability that is incurred from the use or application of contents of this book.

If you purchased this book without a cover you should be aware that this book may have been stolen property and reported as "unsold and destroyed" to the publisher. In this case neither the author nor the publisher has received any payment for this "stripped book."

Dedication

To my family and friends who seems to have been sent here to teach me something about who I am supposed to be. They have nurtured me, challenged me, and even opposed me.... But at every juncture has taught me!

This book is dedicated to my lovely boys, Thomas, Michael and Karl. Teaching them to manage their finance will give them the lives they deserve. They have taught me more about life, presence, and energy management than anything I have done in my life.

Chapter 1: Lean Startup Business Ideas

We are going to look at what it means to be a startup and the process that a startup should follow to ensure success or at least to take a good stab at it.

One of the main premises of this book is that a startup is simply a series of experiments. Experiments that have a hypothesis (an idea to test), limited variables to test (test certain aspects of your idea, not the whole idea at once), and success measurements (how you know when you succeeded or failed). By executing and completing these experiments, you are continually refining and defining your product and target market. Through the experiments, you might find out that no one will buy your product, or that a completely overlooked demographic is actually your target market. In the long run, testing small aspects of your idea will save you time and money because you will be forced to focus on the product that will sell and not on superfluous aspects of your business that do not contribute to your bottom line.

The book is written specifically for SMEs startups, the principles can be and must be applied to social ventures. Here are some examples on how applying the lean start-up principles might look in a small business.

Business idea: Car mechanic

Hypothesis: People want a car mechanic in a convenient location.

Experiment: Find a neighbourhood that has to travel 5 miles to get to a car mechanic. Go door to door and offer to provide basic services at their residence.

Measurements: Get 40 percent of car-owning neighbourhood residents to pay for services.

Why it works? You will be able to determine if a convenient location is a problem. You will start to build a customer base before making the capital investments into a building.

Business idea: Organization services

Hypothesis: People want to get organized because it makes them calm.

Experiment: In the same time frame, send out two sets of marketing materials. One that uses words and colours that reflect calm, peace, tranquillity, etc., and the other that uses words and colours that represent efficiency, time-saving, productivity, etc.

Measurements: Record which marketing materials created the most interest.

Why it works? You will be able to see what motivates people to get organized and develop a customer-centric marketing strategy.

Using the lean startup principles can be intimidating and might be counter intuitive to traditional startup thinking. The fact is you can plan as much as you want but in reality business plans reflect the world that is in your mind, and not the world that actually exists. To start a successful business from the beginning, you need to be in the trenches with your potential customers.

Given that you are in research mode, it is important to embrace some simple processes to ensure the search for a scalable business model is an efficient one. In many ways, these are lessons in hyper efficiency, where time and money is precious and the basis for informed decision making is primarily on the back of building what they call a Minimum Viable Product (MVP). An MVP is a basic version of the product that can be sent to some customers (ideally early adopters) who will give you feedback which will help you decide what to do next.

Rather than building the service and trying it out on customers, create a sign-up page that merely promises to deliver this groundbreaking capability. Then present it to some prospective clients. Compare their enrolment rate with that of a control group shown the usual sign-up page. The results will give you the confidence either to proceed or toss the idea into the circular file. No one would actually get the new feature yet, of course, because it hasn't been built.

In effect we are suggesting that you look for 'evidence of demand' before building the complete product, and an easy way to test for this is to observe real user behaviour on say, a web page. Every click on a button signals intent, regardless of whether or not the product in the back end is there or not, and this data helps you assess likely demand.

Chapter 2: Knowing What it Takes

I am sure we have all dream of doing something on our own, maybe start a restaurant or an antique shop?

As I am cooking some exotic dish in the kitchen for my family, from time to time I do pretend I am standing in the kitchen of my restaurant, entertaining the many people who have been flocking it.

You may have had an idea for starting a business but been hesitant to take the plunge. Irrespective of whether you come from a business family or not, building a business from scratch requires skills and fortitude. However, if you are convinced of your skills and talents and feel they are worth investing in a business, we will tell you what the fundamental requirements are that go into starting a lean business.

There are millions of people the world over who are bursting with ideas for starting a business. However, not many of them sit down and take a long look at whether they have what it takes to be successful entrepreneur.

Some of the important characteristics that all entrepreneurs will need are:
1. **Vision**

You must have the ability to see that far away goal, the ultimate objective. And then, you must be able to clearly express yourself and your ideas to convince others of your vision; like bankers, employees and customers.

2. Discipline

You have to know when to listen and when to talk. When you need to enter a market, how long you need to be there and when you need to quit. You should be disciplined enough to bear the market's ups and downs, instead of panicking at bad news and gloating at good news.

3. Curiosity

You want to know more and more about the world around you. You want to know how things work or how they could possibly work better. You tend to read up more and more about things that fascinate you.

4. Never-say-die attitude

You have the passion to carry through your plans, no matter what the circumstances. You will try to do your very best even in the most challenging situations.

5. Interest in People

Finally, it is people who will matter the most. People as employees who will help you run your business and people as customers who will be buying from you. You always show genuine interest and respect towards all.

Chapter 3: Even Before the Beginning

If you decide you have what it takes to start and run a lean business, next you have to decide on the product or service you would like to offer. And that's not always easy!

Maybe you have already made up your mind and are certain of the kind of enterprise you would like to start. However, chances are that like a majority of others, you may be strongly inclined towards a particular product or service without knowing how to decide one way or the other.

Before you start putting in money, time and your efforts, you have to make sure that your idea for a product or service fits in with the demand and current dynamics of the market. You have to understand that a project as large as complex as this will require a combination of factors; your skills and expertise but also what the consumer expectation is. Which brings us to the question how do you know what customers want?

Here are some ideas to get you started in the right direction. Do not limit yourself to what is listed here but use them as guiding points.

1. Design a well thought out and fairly brief survey which can be given to prospective customers to understand how they feel about

the products and services that you are intending to provide.

2. Speak to retail sellers. What are they looking for and what would make them change suppliers?

3. To get in touch with possible customers, put up an informative website. Compile email lists from talking to people or from visitors to your website.

4. Invest some money and take a booth at a trade show. Prepare prototypes and try to demonstrate how your product or service works. Try to hold some product demonstration at fairs and flea markets.

5. Read all you can about your industry and its performance history including present trends from industry trade magazines, both online and offline. You would also do well to speak to industry insiders both employees and executives.

6. Use information available from various sources to research statistics for your particular industry.

7. Try and speak to other business owners, certainly to those who belong to your industry but also to those who are not. All should be able to point out the pros and cons of entering a particular industry. They will also

provide valuable information about potential pitfalls for those who are just starting their business.

While you may have the right idea to start a lean business, you have to make sure you have the right combination of skills and knowledge to make things happen. You should be aware of your strengths and weaknesses, and how to take advantage of the former and address the latter. Again, we give you here some ways you can go about measuring your readiness for starting a lean start-up.

1. You can come across many tests and quizzes, in books, magazines, seminars or even online which will help you assess your commitment, skills and overall suitability for the business.

2. To be successful in an entrepreneurship you also need to be persistent, prepared and passionate about your work. Ask yourself whether you will be able to handle all the ups and downs of the business not only now when you are enthusiastic about it but even 10 years from now.

3. It is extremely helpful if you have a mentor to help out in different aspects; possibly an experienced businessman who knows the in and outs of the industry and is willing to give you his time, advice and when needed lend a helping hand to the business with his expertise. In fact, most will be more than happy to do some mentoring because their

success would have been partially due to some mentor helping them in the initial stages.

4. A businessperson needs to take care of many aspects of the enterprise like planning, working on a strategy, sales and marketing, supplies and procurement, finance and personnel, tax and legal matters. It is not unusual if you feel overwhelmed by the number of things that you need to be taking care of you may also feel that you lack the necessary qualifications or capabilities to handle all the above. However, keep in mind that there are a number of sources where you can find help. You could visit schools and colleges, look up books and websites; even approach Government agencies to get some help in the areas you most need.

5. The best way to start a business is to probably do so with a partner. You will be able to motivate each other, take care of fields you are skilled at and share responsibilities. However, before you start a business with a partner or partners, you better have a clear understanding with them. Make sure they understand what the outcomes may be, that all have the same level of commitment to and expectations about the business. Ensure you have a partnership agreement that will clearly state what the responsibilities and obligations of each partner will be as also what are the ways that a partner can move our or even the

entire partnership dissolved, if in the future there arise certain irreconcilable differences.

Chapter 4: Research the Market

It is very important that you do a thorough research of the market before you venture into your own business. You can find many examples of would-be entrepreneurs standing outside stores and malls speaking to customers or perhaps offering them samples of their products to get their reaction. Many invest in developing some prototypes and send out samples with promotional brochures to trade magazines, potential suppliers and customers and requesting for feedback. Whichever method you choose, what is important is that you test your market for the possible benefits and pitfalls.

Granted, testing a market is tough work. It is going to take some courage to go meet complete strangers and ask them for their opinions. However, there can be no doubt that the best way of beginning a business is to get to know all that you can about your industry. Till you do the groundwork, what you are resting on is your instinctive confidence about your product or service, which may or may not be right.

Only a first-hand and thorough market research will reveal whether your instincts are in the right direction or not. In fact, most entrepreneurs seem to overlook this very basic but fundamental requirement placing unflinching confidence in their idea. While confidence is good, misplaced confidence can be foolhardy. In fact, it is estimated that only one fourth of all businesses carry out any kind of market research and that this could be a big factor in many small businesses failing.

In fact, instead of spending too much time and money in an extensive market research, experts suggest that you carry out this in stages.

Stage 1:

SWOT analysis: This will bring out your business's strengths, weaknesses, opportunities and threats. If the results at this stage suggest that there are enough opportunities, you can then move on to carrying out more thorough primary and secondary research.

Stage 2:

Primary Research: This involves a lot of legwork. It means getting off computers and books and actually going into stores and shops, trying to gain an understanding of your product or service will be received. You have to go into the field to find out what prospective customers, suppliers and yes, even competitors think of your idea.

    a.   You could find many consultants who will carry out this research for you but you may find it worthwhile to carry out the exercise yourself. Also, the contacts you develop during this phase can help you carry your business forward.

    b.   Try meeting as many people in the industry as you can. They will be in a great position to give you some solid advice about the industry.

    c.   You could also speak to potential suppliers about the current scenarios in the market and where they feel they need help the most. Try and understand where the gap in the market is where your product or service will fit the best.

d. Another good source of information may be non-competing but similar businesses in other areas. They could give you valuable advice and guidance.

e. You could also try speaking to businesses selling products and services closely related to what you are trying to do. For example if you are trying to enter the business of hand-made shawls, you could speak to businesses dealing in custom shoes or hand-made scarves. They could provide advice as well as referrals to potential customers.

f. Potential customers are by far the most important part of primary research. In fact, experts say, you have to attack this potential source like a guerrilla. Be tough and get as many names to speak to. Try and understand who will be most interested in your services or products and what features they are looking for.

g. Many entrepreneurs stand outside of malls and stores trying hard to speak to sympathetic customers to understand what they are buying and why they are buying them. If lucky, they will even be willing to try a sample of your product. It is absolutely essential that you get into the field, speak to as many people as you can and get as much of honest feedback as you can. You should ask tough questions and find out what customers think of your product. Will they buy it or wont they buy it? If they won't buy it, why won't they buy it? Will they buy it at a different price? Get all the complaints and warnings that you can find. It is better that you hear all the negative feedback now before you start so that you can take corrective measures if possible or at the worst, dump the project before putting in more money.

h. Another very useful tool to consider is focus groups and surveys. Focus Groups are just a group of potential customers all gathered in one place and who will provide you with actual qualitative answers on the good and bad sides of a product or service as also their opinion on what could be done to improve them.

i. You have to learn to be objective while dealing with focus groups so it may be best to bring in a professional facilitator who will know how to conduct a focus group, ask specific questions and knows how to listen. Ideally, one should try to get as large a focus group as possible. For example, as a thumb of rule, if you were aiming at a market for 100,000 consumers, a good focus group would have about 400-500 in your focus group so that the results can be statistically significant.

j. You use the latest technological innovations to your benefit by using online polls to the same effect. Create an informative, promotional website with a complete, helpful description of your product and then ask for feedback from visitors. You could also ask all your friends, family members and colleagues to take the survey and to reply honestly to the questions asked. Get more visitors to your website by sponsoring ads on related websites or newsletters.

Stage 3:

Secondary Research: This means moving away from the market and getting information from sources such as trade journals and magazines where you can find published papers, directories and even market statistics. You can collect useful qualitative data in terms of urban population, trade association figures, government and industry forecasts and white papers as well as research reports from experts such as securities analysts. All these will help you figure out, what are the current dynamics of the market, what are the growth prospects, where could the risks lie and what would the potential be for your new product and service.

Chapter 5: Business Start-up Legal Requirements

When you start playing a game of Scrabble or Monopoly, the first thing you do is to organize all the letters or the money. Similarly, when you start on a business, you need to get organized and have all your paperwork in order. There are going to be many Government rules and regulations that you may need to follow. It is important that you understand business start-up legal structure including registering the business name. If you show carelessness towards any of these, you could be in for a nasty surprise in the future.

Legal Structure

This is one of the main aspects that any business owner needs to resolve before getting started. Would you like to start a sole proprietorship or go into a partnership? Or would you like to start an incorporated company? Before you decide on which is best, understand the implications of each option.

In a sole proprietorship, only one person is the owner of the business and the business has no formal legal existence of its own. As a result, all the profits go to the owner and he also bears all the losses. This is the simplest form of business and its simplicity is one of its advantages. However, all the debt that falls on a business has to be repaid by the owner.

A partnership can consist of two more partners. The business again has no legal status and the profits are just divided among the partners in a previously agreed upon manner or based on the investment that each partner has contributed.

However, many businesses prefer to become incorporated (i.e. Limited liability), as that gives their business a legal status separate from their owner's. This allows them to keep the profits and liabilities separate from that of their owners.

Registering a business name

Once you have chosen the kind of structure you want to have, you have to decide what name you would like for your business. You may want to select your name and have it registered fairly early so that there are no regulations problems later or worry about a competitor stealing your name. Most of the time, registering a business name is done at the state level but you should check what rules apply in your Country.

Check out what licensing you need

Most businesses need to apply for some kind of local license to be able to conduct a business in their community. Of course, there are exceptions like home-based businesses. But it is more than likely that if yours is not a home-based business, it will require a license. Make sure you check about what other land and zoning regulations you need to comply, by speaking with local authorities.

Tax Requirements

In all probability you will need to apply to the Inland Revenue for tax number, which will allow you to start charging small business taxes.

Complying with Regulations

You need to stay in touch with your lawyer and your accountant to first set up the business in accordance with all the regulations. Later, they will also help maintain your business records so that there is regular compliance from your end with the existing laws and regulations.

Chapter 6: Business Plan

We now come to probably the most feared, most avoided but the most important task in beginning a business. Many believe that a business plan is only for those seeking outside financial help like from a bank or investors.

Others believe that this is just unnecessary paperwork and that the best business plan is in their heads. Some who believe in it do so only half-heartedly and come up with a one or two page plan of how they see their business progressing. All these approaches are misguided and without proper direction, the business is more likely to sink than grow.

The most important point to remember about a business plan is that it is first and foremost for you! It is to layout a concrete plan to successfully start, manage and then grow your company. It will force you to think and invest in strategy planning, market research, financial planning, operational details and marketing plans.

However, we will concede that it is not easy to immediately start out working on a business plan and every business plan will need working and reworking. We will try to provide you first with some general guidelines on what a good business plan should include and once we have you thinking in that direction, we will start helping you fill out all the details in the business plan.

Let us first outline what a well written business plan will contain

1. An attractive statement of purpose – when people ask you what your business does, this is the first statement you will be using.
2. Complete description of who you believe your customers will be any special niche you are aiming for as well as a general strategy for winning over that niche.
3. Complete description of your product or service. Mention what are the highlights and what could be its challenges, production or selling wise.
4. A well compiled list of people who will be working with you or advising you in various aspects. Mention clearly what their skills and areas of expertise are.
5. Details of financial plans that will show how you plan to finance the first few years and expected revenues and expenses
6. Major risks that you may face before your business settles down and major advantages that may help it grow well.

As you can see, your business plan is more like a map to guide you through, at any point in time. If you have given sufficient thought to planning and written down the steps in sufficient detail in your business plan, no matter how many ups or downs there are, you should be able to stay on course. In fact, one of my mentors likes to compare a business plan to the centre board of a sailboat. Irrespective of how the wind is blowing, your business plan will always help you stay on course, headed in the right direction.

If you would like to look at some samples before you begin on one, you can speak to banks or business link, which can help you by showing samples of a few business plans. You could also look up one of the thousands of books in your local library, which should contain a sample. However, treat the sample as just that. It is meant to give you an idea of what are the essentials that should go in a business plan. Do not worry if your plan is too long or short, simple or complicated. What should matter to you is that it is written in a manner that you can follow easily, contains information that is helpful to your business, identified possible challenges that could arise and outlined plans for overcoming them.

Some entrepreneurs who were new to the business world did not have the skills or knowledge that would be required to start and run the business. They used the business plan to understand what aspects of the company they need to know and know well. Like production or pricing, selling and distribution. They used the business plan as a guide to learning all the relevant topics for one year and this helped them to launch a successful business at the end of it.

For those who already have some skills and knowledge, a business plan works to guide them in one consistent direction. It is a to-do list that tells you what you need to be doing at regular intervals.

Using your business plan, you can use various sources of information to gather statistics, study competitors and gain knowledge about production and pricing. As you work on your business plan you will understand better how your business can function well and how it can actually make money. You will be able to analyze markets, costs and prices. All these can be used effectively in planning your financial statements and estimates of revenue for the future. Knowing so much about your business gives you great confidence but you are also able to convince others more easily of the feasibility of your business.

You will therefore derive multiple benefits from your business plan; you will be able to have a detailed plan which will help overcome potential problems. Your grip on the financials of the business will help convince bankers and investors to put in money for your business. Further, your market research will pay dividends for many years to come and can be used to convince retailers as well as potential investors.

So do not ever catch yourself thinking that you are too busy planning other aspects of your business and that you do not have enough time to work on a business plan. Never fool yourself into thinking that if you have a good idea, the money and the enthusiasm, you will be able to start a business. Planning is so important that if you are not willing to focus on the most important issues like strategy and operating details, then you should be asking yourself if you are up to running a business.

Chapter 7: Essential Elements of a Good Business Plan

Hopefully, we have convinced you in the previous chapter that every business needs a business plan; though the format and content will vary from business to business. However, there will be some common topics and questions asked of every business, the answers to which will go in your business plan.

Your company profile: You will need to give details of your business, the products it intends to sell, details of the legal structure and key employees.

Market outlook: What is the market you are aiming at, what do you perceive will be its present size, future growth, trends and opportunities?

Product/Service Description: What is the USP of your product or service and what may be its challenges? What makes it better than your competitors'?

Operational Details: Where are you planning to produce your product? Where will you be selling it? What are the distribution networks like? What are the risks involved?

Marketing Plan: What market are you aiming at; do you have a niche area? How will you sell your USP to prospective buyers? How will competitors react and are you prepared to counter-react?

Sales Plan: Who will be helping you sell your products? Would you be providing any incentive for them to do so?

Financial Statements: These will contain details of how you plan to finance your business till it starts making profits. Include carefully calculated sales and profits projections along with monthly cash flows.

Main risk factors: You should be able to think about potential risks and threats that your business may face down the road. How do you plan on overcoming them and still ensuring your business is on track?

This is just the outline of what should go into a business plan. You now need to take time, study each aspect carefully and make sure you understand it carefully before putting down details in your business plan. You have to particularly ensure that you have given thought to every key challenge that your business may face and noted down how you intend to cope with them and ensure that the business is not affected drastically even under those circumstances. This level of detailed planning will be crucial in convincing a banker or any potential investor for whom your business plan is all that they will know about you.

These details will also help you many a times when you need to remind yourself of what you should be doing to keep the business on track.

Chapter 8: The Devil is in the Details

We will now try and help you work on the details of some crucial aspects of the business plan that we had mentioned in previous chapter. Make sure you have enough information in those areas that are particularly relevant to your business.

Describe Your Business

You have to be very clear about the business that you are in, the exact market that you will be aiming at and how your business is going to be structured. You should mention very quickly the mission of your business in subjective terms as well objective terms using hard figures. Mention details of products, focusing on their benefits to customers and emphasizing on what makes them different from others. In fact, that is the only way your business can grow; if you think of your product and service as something that your customers and the market needs and wants rather that what you are interested in producing or selling.

Talk Up Your Team

Next to you, your team is the most important aspect of your business. If you believe that they lend you that special competitive edge, explain why fully giving details of their qualifications and skills as also their industry related expertise. You will also need to explain what other important job positions you intend to provide and how you are planning on looking for people. And of course, you will also need to emphasize your own qualifications and skills for running this business.

Operational Details

While a broad business plan is good enough to get you started, you will need a detailed operational plan to keep your business going from day to day without any problems. By including operational details, you will be showing that you have a good grasp of the business requirements and that you have given sufficient thought to the entire production process, reducing the chances for errors and providing for meeting any challenges should one arise. These will include production, distribution, selling and marketing details as also what are the main and alternate sources of supplies. In this increasingly technological age, you should consider and mention how you will effectively use technology to substantially reduce costs and increase productivity.

Marketing Plan

What kind of distribution avenues will your business be using? What methods have you used to decide the pricing of the product, and how do you intend to promote and advertise it? Would you use only traditional modes of distribution and advertising or would you make use of the Internet and ecommerce?

Sales Plan

You will need to include sales projections and revenues and then explain why you are confident that these will come true. Try to defend your expected revenue figures by describing how you plan to convince likely prospects or key distributors to buy. It is important to show that you have given this enough thought, that you have ways of convincing retailers and customers to buy your products and also of how your sales team will be working to make this succeed.

Risk Assessment

The most important detail to include in any business plan not only to assure investors that you are working to keep their investment safe and growing but also to make sure that you give enough consideration to all possible risk factors and have plans to mitigate each one of these. You may need to guard against economic downturns, bankruptcy of a key customer, employee issues and so on. Take nothing for granted.

Along with knowing how to write a business plan, you should also know what you have to avoid in a business plan? Here are a few aspects that you may need to be careful about while working on a business plan.

1. Never confuse delusion with optimism

It is okay to overestimate your sales projections and underestimate your costs. However, you have to do so within the realm of reality. Proposing profit margins of 80% in the first year is most certainly a delusion. Not only does this mean that you do not understand the way a business works but this will most certainly ensure that no banker takes you seriously. To ensure that your financial projections are taken seriously, stay honest but optimistic and back up all your figures.

2. Choose a small initial target market

Do not aim to provide a wide variety of products or services or in a very large market. You are more likely to get lost; concentrate your resources in a small market. Focus your efforts on establishing this business first.

3. Clearly identify your first few target customers

Mention clearly how you plan to reach them and how you intend to be successful in selling your product or service to them.

4. Emphasize your unique selling point

Highlight in enough number of places how your product or service is different from those in the market so far. Make enough use of bullet points and short, descriptive paragraphs so that your points come out loud and clear.

5. Perfect your executive summary

Work hard on your executive summary. It will convey in very brief all that you need to convey about your business. Make it authoritative, keep it to the point and make it convincing. What makes it all the more important is that this may be the only part of the entire business plan that an investor may actually read.

Chapter 9: Managing Finance

It is very important that you have sufficient interest in finances and enough knowledge of finances before you even start your own business. In fact, this is one important factor of why small businesses fail so much; they don't adequately know how to control costs or make proper collections and not let debts grow beyond an unreasonable limit.

For countless entrepreneurs, the major stumbling blocks in starting a business are forecasting sales, compiling financial statements and projecting regular cash-flows. Of course, there are accountants who will help you with the nitty-gritty of things but you have to at some point be able to have a global picture of what your finances are like and where you are headed. In fact, it is thought that the reason out of thousands of firms launched every year, only a few survive. Those that do not are ones wherein the owners did not have a good understanding of what their expected revenues, would be or how they related to the expenses and profit.

Only a lucky few can start their business in this world with unlimited finances. Therefore making financial forecasts allows prospective entrepreneurs, to estimate how much time will be needed for the business to settle down, reach a break-even point and then actually start making profits. Most investors and experts believe that it is best to prepare financial forecasts of at least two to three years which will include profit and loss statement for all years and monthly cash-flows for at least one year. These forecasts will help you get a reality check in terms of where you stand with the money and what you will need to do to fund the business till it starts making profits. You may need to consider various options of finding the money including using your own resources, asking a partner to pitch in with some investment or speaking to family or friends who can lend you some money. For large sums it is best to approach a bank. You could also try other investors and specialty loan programs.

Financial forecasts also serve another important function. Working on these details will help you realize the true costs of starting and running a business. You will be able to judge for yourself on whether you will be able to build a self-sustaining business with the kind of financial projections that you anticipate or should you just cancel the project instead of wasting more time and efforts in it. Do not delude yourself into thinking that your business will start flourishing in its very first year. Even if your projections are showing that, redo them and then make sure you are honest and realistic about sales projections and cost estimates. If your projections show that you are losing a lot of money in your first year, then you need to look where you can reduce your spending and how you can reduce your fixed costs.

Either way, your financial planning has allowed you to know your business better and made you stronger.

Chapter 10: Tips on Financial Planning

We will provide you with some solid tips on how to get started on your financial planning.

Forecasting Sales

How many products do you think you will sell in your first year? No, you do not know. Nobody knows. In fact, business planning is not meant to provide instant answers; it is supposed to reduce uncertainty.

Carry out a primary market research. Understand what your market is and how big your particular segment is. Understand how interested potential customers are which will provide your sales forecast with lots of credibility. Meet with people in the industry and maybe competitors from other areas to get a real idea of what pricing trends are like, how seasonal variations affect sales and typical order patterns.

It is believed that many new entrepreneurs hope that they will capture a certain percentage of the market which maybe 5% or 10% and base their sales forecast on this. On the other hand, old hands will tell you that only a small percentage of a market is willing to change and so your sales forecast may be off by as much as 50%.

Experts claim that at times, at the very beginning, you may need to sell about $80,000 worth of products to make $40,000 in profit. And this may still be considered a good target. While there is no one right answer, it is always good to have some kind of objective in mind. You may be best served by breaking up your financial forecasts into monthly forecasts adjusting them to account for seasonal variations. This will help you focus on the targets month by month at the beginning and also to track what caused any dip or rise in sales that month.

Learn to Calculate Costs

While forecasting sales involves a lot of guesswork and most of it is based on instinctive feelings about the market, calculating costs is a more simple forward exercise. It is just a matter of basic math; you add the cost of producing and operating and you have the costs of production. You just need to consider all the inputs that will go into the product before it is ready to be sold and then add them up; that will give the cost of the product or service.

Your inputs may be rent, advertising, and salaries. Of course, these are over and above the actual cost of production like space, raw materials, labour and so on. To ensure that you get the best deal on all supplies and services, make a few phone calls to understand where you can get good quotes on rent, equipment and supplies. Though it may sound more costly, try not to engage in long-term, fixed price contracts which will allow you small business to stay flexible and keep open options of buying from cheaper outlets in the future.

If you would like to see whether the pricing of your product is compatible with the costs you are incurring, you can use many of the business costs and performance comparison tools being provided increasingly by governments.

Cash Flow Projections

Revenues do not always mean cash. In fact, most customers who buy will take anywhere from 20 to 90 days to make cash payment. That brings in the issue of cash flow. While your customer may need so many days to pay, your cash requirements will still be in force. To provide for those days when you may face a potential cash threat, it is very important that you have your cash flow projections ready.

To understand what may cause these problems start by speaking to people in the industry. Speak to suppliers and other veterans. Make sure you account for the industry practice into the cash-flow forecasts. For example, if the average payment that is made by a customer is only after 45 days you may need to go for almost two months without any cash coming in for that particular sale. And if you have a large portion of fixed costs coming in sometime then, you are going to have a serious cash crunch, which will affect your business.

Chapter 11: Lets Go on a Treasure Hunt

The following analogy has been often repeated for business plan. As your business plan provides an overall structure and strategy for your business, it is like a treasure map. However, it is your marketing plan that will clearly outline how you will be able to reach those goals in your business, making it the key to the treasure chest.

Again, a marketing plan is something that is not sufficiently given thought to by most new entrepreneurs. Either they are in a hurry for their product or service to hit the market or they are just unaware of what impact it can have on the growth of business. A marketing plan is an incredibly powerful tool, but it turns out to be useful if you have taken the efforts and come up with correct information about markets, pricing and the sales pitch. Since these are issues that are bound to come up in the future, by having a plan you are not only anticipating them but also using them to get a head start.

A marketing plan will also help you to focus. You will know what market to concentrate on, what products to concentrate on (at least at the beginning) and how to deal with problems in those specific areas. Thus the plan helps you to concentrate in areas where the business is doing well.

However, a marketing plan is never achieved in one go. You will have to keep coming back as you gain insight from various sources, like in conversation with customers or industry insiders. As you gain more perspective, come and add a few more lines to your marketing plan till you reach a stage where you think the plan is reasonably complete.

What should your marketing plan be like? Consider some of the following, which will help you to at least get started right away.

Product Strategy

1. Make sure you give enough details about your product or service, what unique requirement is it planning to meet, and what makes them superior to the competitors'.

2. You have to clearly identify which is your target market (identify common characteristics like, age, income and education) Outline your product or service, the needs it meets and what makes it superior to the competition.

3. How long will these customers buy from you? Common products and services may be challenged by a new entrant sooner. If you are dealing with customized scarves, chances are your customers will be very loyal to your business.

4. Try and understand what the size of the market is and what its growth prospects like.

How does your product or service fit in with this growth? Is there any particular niche you are trying to capture? What are your shot-term and long-term goals to do so? Write down clearly all your observations and what has led you to come to the conclusion. This should include your observations from the primary and secondary market research carried out before.

5. Explain clearly why customers will be buying your product or service which will then lead to where, who and more importantly how often they will do so. Also include competitors with their products and services for comparison. Draw a direct comparison so as to bring out the advantages of your product or service clearly including your pricing strategy and how it compares better to the competitors' pricing. Even if your pricing is a little higher than other competitors, make a case for why your product or service is still superior.

Marketing Strategy

1. Your marketing strategy has to be laid for not one or two but possibly for three years. Identify what the individual strategies will be like; would you go in for direct marketing and media advertising, how about Internet marketing, will you be considering trade promotion or public relations?

2. If you need to produce some promotional materials then which ones will you be laying emphasis on, and how many will you produce? Where will you focus on?

3. What is your website strategy like? Would you be using it only for advertising or also for selling? Is the website informational and complete enough?

4. What will your customer relationship management strategy be like (CRM)?

5. Where will you concentrate your initial marketing efforts and why. What are the key marketing message that should be used there?

6. Marketing strategy will also involve building a marketing calendar that will specify all the marketing opportunities and resources to make sure those efforts are successful.

Sales Strategy

Your marketing efforts may convince people about your product and convince investors that there are enough potential customers. However now is when your sales strategy will step in to help customers make up their minds finally in favour of your products and services.

1. You need to include the key members of your sales team, which will include everyone, involved in sales.

2. Describe their qualifications, skills and what especially makes them capable of handling sales in this industry.

3. Give particular mention to sales team leaders and what effective leaders they are.

4. What would be the mode of sale and what would the cost of the added functionality. Would you be selling through traditional avenues like sales agents, over the phone, selling to retailers and so on?

5. Write how you plan to reward and motivate your sales team

6. Also mention what special features like warranties, guarantees or service commitments you will be able to offer to customers.

You can get started on your marketing plan by reading up on books or articles or even getting information online. You could enrol for a college course or seminar to get information and guidance on producing these plans. The most important thing still remains the execution of the plan and to do so, every member of you team needs to be aware of what they are responsible for.

Chapter 12: Hiring Tips for Lean Startup

There is to do list when you are first starting a company. Each co-founder or employee executes several job descriptions jumbled together, and it seems a simple solution to just hire a new person and delegate away responsibilities, never to be worried about it again. This becomes especially relevant post-funding, because it suddenly becomes plausible to hire with the intended result of getting more done faster.

But this is not necessarily true, because as you add people to a team or project, there is increase in communications overhead that makes everyone slightly less productive.

It may seem counterintuitive to do anything slow when following lean startup methods, but this point stands. To continue executing effectively, you must not introduce a point of friction to your team. Finding the right person is paramount, and worth the wait.

Don't Hire Too Soon

When you first think you need to hire someone, write a detailed job description. It is not enough to have a problem that you don't think someone on your team can solve. That often leads to imagining that your new recruit will bring magical powers with them. At this point, if you don't really understand the problem, how will you choose the right person to take it on? A killer job description will help you understand what tasks you need done and whether it really justifies another full-time employee.

When I was just starting out and still bootstrapping, I approached a good friend to join me. Within a few months, it became clear that it was too early I did not have a job for anyone yet, and I had put the cart in front of the horse therefore I would like to recommend that someone in the company take on a job before hiring an outside person to do it. This helps you understand if the new job is truly critical, and if so, will make integrating a new person into the team faster, because an existing employee will understand the problem and have credibility around it.

Use Your Personal Connections

The people you have worked with before are a lower risk because they will integrate into your team easier, and you already know their strengths and weaknesses. Take an inventory of people you know who are awesome at what they do, and ask yourself, "Why is this person not working for my startup?"

Do a Practice Run

We recommend giving your best candidate a small, non-critical task to work on to see how they solve problems and communicate with the team. Other companies invite a person in to work with them for a day and follow it up by going out for drinks.

At one of the companies I use to work for; we have had engineers in for a day of coding before going out for beers with the team, which really adds up to give us a full picture of the candidate. At the end of the day, we all ask ourselves whether this is someone we did be excited to see every morning. If not, it is a no go. This allows you to test for the culture fit that is so critical with a small team.

To be able to pick the right people and make use of their abilities effectively, here are more rules you need to be aware of:

1. Always make sure you have an eye for the best talent. Understand their potential clearly and then measure the results. Have reasonable expectations.

2. Try and create an environment where hard-working employees are respected and rewarded while those who lag behind are given enough motivation to start performing well.

3. Make sure you look well enough and you look hard enough. Keep even your friends, family friends and customers aware that you are looking for help. Use traditional methods of advertising as in local newspapers as well as online job boards and industry websites. Try trades shows and radio shows. You could try

offering a finders' fee or referral fee to people who refer you to good qualified candidates.

4. You should know your business well and that means you should know perfectly well what kind of skills and experience you will be looking for in people. It will also tell you the kind of personal attitudes and values you are looking for in the people you are looking to hire. It is this kind of clarity that will bring top performers to you business. Many people like to join a business that they can feel loyal to, that they can feel a part of.

5. You need to provide detailed job descriptions. It is your job because you as the head of the business have an overall picture of what kind of jobs positions will be required for a smooth functioning of the business. You will be able to specify what are the skills, qualifications, education, level of passion and commitment that you desire in an applicant.

6. Never hurry up an interview. Take at least one hour to speak to the applicants. An interview is never a one-way process; you are trying to gauge them just as they are trying to gauge you. Just as you are taking time to see if they are suitable for your business, they are taking time to see what your business has to offer them. So, be amply prepared with a list of question, take notes of all the candidates and ask specific questions. Questions about their skills, industry knowledge, their perceived

strengths and weaknesses. Allow them to answer some more general question like 'How would you handle a situation like ...' or 'If your colleague is behaving like this, how would you handle it?"

7. Make sure you explain clearly what is expected of them. Especially for those coming in from large corporate houses, where all responsibilities are shared and hence less to bear, in a small business, a lot is expected of the employees. This is doubly so in a small start-up. Make sure you tell them what their main responsibilities will be but also make it clear that they may be expected to work in other areas. This way there will be less chance of feeling let down or over-burdened.

8. When you offer a person a job, you are not looking for just an employee. You are looking at growth prospects and how that person may grow with the business. This means he may need to take up other responsibilities. You need to understand if the person is up to that. A small business cannot afford too many people who can do only one job albeit very competently. People who can do multitasking are more valued in small businesses.

9. It always helps to give new people as much pre-job training as possible. If new hires receive more training and guidance, they are likely to be more successful and in turn will contribute more to the business. Even if not a

full pre-job training, consider putting them with older and more experienced employees who can take a few weeks to break in the new employees.

10. If you set goals for employees and motivate them to achieve them, it will boost their self-confidence and at the same time help the business to prosper. Make sure the goals are SMART goals (Specific, Measurable, Achievable, Realistic and Time-based).

11. Keep reviewing their progress regularly and provide specific feedback so that they can improve. Reward employees who have performed above average and also those who have shown significant progress. Wherever possible connect compensation with results achieved so that the business does well whenever the employee does well.

12. Take extra efforts in making sure that employees feel appreciated and part of the business. Try to be as democratic in processes as possible, encourage new ideas and initiatives. Ensure that the workplace is full of fun, positive and no nasty gossip is indulged in. As a small business you may not be able to offer a full range of benefits; try and compensate by offering the odd bonus, paid training courses and seminar and additional days off.

13. Maintain free and frank communication with employees and never play favourites. Similarly encourage honest feedback even about you.

Puts together a hiring team that debriefs after each round of interviews; this active forum will enables each member to voice opinions on each candidate, and they are able to keep standards high, asking, why is this person perfect for your business? Relying on intuition will help you cut down on mistakes.

Finally, remember how difficult hiring mistakes are to undo. The typical cost of a hiring mistake is three times an employee's annual salary and benefits, couple that with the human element and emotional drag of removing a piece of your team, even as it proves ineffective, and that should be sufficient incentive to hire intentionally and with hesitation, for the eventual win.

Chapter 13: The Way forward

Many entrepreneurs have a thirst for knowledge and information. They would like to know how things work and how they can be made to work better. They would like to seek inspiration in different places and look for solutions in the most unlikely of places. It is this spirit of enterprise that leads them to start their own business hoping to start something unique.

However, there are a lot of different things that one needs to know about while starting, managing and growing a business. You need to know so many tricks and loopholes, so many people and resources so that you can face the challenges when you meet them. However there is no way you will ever be aware of all the potential pitfalls that face you as you go your way. That is why many more business owners; both well established as well as newcomers, prefer to look for help from industry advisors and mentors.

Often the kind of information that you are looking for as your business is growing gradually is not the kind that is locally available. You may need to seek advice from other national or even international contacts to help deal with unexpected. Though it is unusual, requests are entertained and solutions suggested. However not everyone has to call someone halfway across the country to get a quick solution to a problem.

There are many peer groups formed of young entrepreneurs who help members bring their individual experiences to the table. They can share their problems and also learn from each other's experiences. Business clubs and associations often hold regular forums to bring together members so that there can be shared meetings and activities. Local chamber of commerce can set up formal mentoring programs or advisors. One can also find business and/or life coaches whose main job is to help you find the answers to your questions. They will help you in crucial areas such as time-management or delegating, prioritizing or finding your own way forward.

A good mentor is an invaluable asset. Not only can he help you deal with immediate problems like staff unrest or marketing problems, nut also help you deal with long term challenges. Such as what should the emphasis on the product be and what should the sale strategy be. Mentors can also put you in touch with lawyers, accountants or sympathetic investors. They can do the important job of spreading the word when you are finding the right person for a job. Their single most function may be to provide with moral support; they will pull you through your worst crisis by offering words of guidance and motivation.

Forward or back to the beginning?

So you have survived the toughest phase of your business. This phase has challenged you physically, mentally and emotionally. Your creativity, resourcefulness, trust and initiative have all been tested and you have come out with flying colours. However, this is just the beginning of your business.

Now you need to carry forward what you have started and grow your business.

Obviously business cannot be static. Whether it is a small store at the corner or a large ecommerce website, your business is always active. It needs to remain so and to grow; it needs to get sharper and smarter. While this may not seem a concern as you may still be basking in the glory of your success, remember it does not take long for competitors to catch up and then it will not be long before your customers start moving away.

Many experts believe that most entrepreneurs tend to work 'in' their business as opposed to on their business. The business is built around their specific skills and is reflective more of what they can offer. Once they lose interest in the business, the business is doomed to failure. However, there are the more successful entrepreneurs who work 'on' the business. Their goal is to provide customers superior products and services. These entrepreneurs take the time to develop skills for themselves and their staff, build on customer relationships and technological know-how and establish an organization where the entire staff works for the comfort of the customer.

If you have successfully launched your business and are now aiming at upgrading and growing your business, consider some key areas to focus on. Remember these activities need to be done on a regular basis and not when you believe you will find time for them.

Always keep working on your business plan

The business plan is a guideline for the regular functioning of your business. Based on your experiences so far, update your plan with new financial projections, new details about your product service and possibly new job positions.

Work on an operations manual

Let your employees know how your business works and what are that standards that are expected from all employees.

Keep an eye on new sources of growth

An idea for expanding a business cannot be implemented in one day. In fact if you are keen on growing, you need to be on the lookout for openings that may suggest new sources of work. However, under no circumstances should the current clients be affected. Obviously, it is unfair that your current clients are affected because you would like to expand. Secondly, you need to be extra careful of your reputation now.

Understand your customers' needs

A recent survey by a computer-security firm tried to sell their products recently to a new set of customers along with the old. When a comparison was made as to who made the most purchases, they turned out to be old customers. This shows that better results may be achieved by understanding the result of present customer and gradually trying to increase the market. Try and listen to your current customer a little more. You may want to get more feedback from them and now how you can improve your product and service.

Maintain your network

Always maintain contact with your lawyer, accountant, banker and mentor. Take the effort of updating them with developments in your business.

Consider exporting

If you have already established yourself well here then why not consider sending your product to other countries. You could try by understanding the markets in other countries also how you can establish relations with local customers and distributors. With global payment systems in place, you can export products easily.

Training

Your business is well settled now and may be at a stage where it is ready of take off. However, this means the current batch of employees will need to be retrained to handle the pressures of new responsibilities. Try to keep them motivated by letting them be in charge of new project and letting them travel.

Keep a ready source

Your growing business will need more resources to keep pace and to track what the competition is doing. Try to bring in new and fresh marketing idea, try out new products and build on a list of prospective customers.

Build a company culture

All your employees should know your values and ideals and through implementation of regular, well-thought policies; you can create a business culture that actually values integrity, hard work and customer service.

Never stop learning

Never give up your curiosity and never give up learning. You will never be able to fully master the art of enterprise management if you cannot understand important aspects of leadership and employee motivation, time management, marketing, finance and selling. Make sure you have an open mind on them and read all you can from magazines and books, seminars and course or of course from industry experts.

Maintain good credit rating

Maintain a good credit rating with your banker. Make sure you ask him for more credit when things are going well so that payments are prompt and your credit rating goes up.

Understand the outreach of the Internet

Technological innovations especially on the Internet front are really changing the way we do business. Understand what application can be made use of to grow your business. Try blogs, newsletters, webinars, ecommerce auctions and podcasts to learn how best you can grow your business by exploiting the full potential of the Internet.

Chapter 14: Keep it Lean

The Lean Startup relies on validated learning, scientific experimentation, and iterative product releases to shorten product development cycles, measure progress, and gain valuable customer feedback. In this way, companies, especially startups, can design their products or services to meet the demands of their customer base without requiring large amounts of initial funding or expensive product launches.

Originally developed with high-tech companies in mind, the lean startup philosophy has since been expanded to apply to any individual, team, or company looking to introduce new products or services into the market. Today, the lean startup's popularity has grown outside of its Silicon Valley birthplace and has spread throughout the world.

Ries developed the idea for the Lean Startup from his experiences as a startup advisor, employee, and founder. His first startup, Catalyst Recruiting, failed because they did not understand the wants of their target customers, and because they focused too much time and energy on the initial product launch.

After Catalyst, Ries was a senior software engineer with There, Inc. Ries describes There Inc. as a classic example of a Silicon Valley startup with five years of stealth R&D, $40 million in financing, and nearly 200 employees at the time of product launch. In 2003, There, Inc. launched its product, There.com, but they were unable to garner popularity beyond the initial early adopters. Ries claims that despite the many proximate causes for failure, the most important mistake was that the company's "vision was almost too concrete," making it impossible to see that their product did not accurately represent consumer demand.

Although the lost money differed by orders of magnitude, the failures of There, Inc. and Catalyst Recruiting share similar origins, with Ries stating that "it was working forward from the technology instead of working backward from the business results you are trying to achieve. Ries began to develop the lean startup philosophy from these experiences, and from others observed by working in the high-tech entrepreneurial world.

The lean startup philosophy is based on lean manufacturing, the streamlined production philosophy developed in the 1980s by Japanese car manufacturers. The lean manufacturing system considers the expenditure of resources for any goal other than the creation of value for the end customer and waste elimination. In particular, the system focuses on strategically placing small stockpiles of inventory, known as kanban, throughout the assembly line as opposed to storing a full stock in a centralized warehouse. These kanban provide production workers with the necessary inputs to production as they need them, and in so doing, reduce waste while increasing productivity. Additionally, immediate quality control checkpoints can identify mistakes or imperfections during assembly as early as possible to ensure that the least amount of time is expended developing a faulty product.

Another primary focus of the lean management system is to maintain close connections with suppliers in order to understand their customers' desires.

Similar to the precepts of lean management, lean startup philosophy seeks to eliminate wasteful practices and increase value producing practices during the product development phase so that startups can have better chances of success without requiring large amounts of outside funding, elaborate business plans, or the perfect product.

we believes that customer feedback during product or service development is integral to the lean startup process, and ensures that the producer does not invest time designing features or services that consumers do not want. This is done primarily through two processes, using key performance indicators and a continuous deployment process. Because startups typically cannot afford to have their entire investment depend upon the success of one single product or service launch, we maintains that by releasing a minimum viable product or service that is not yet finalized, the company can then make use of customer feedback to help further tailor their product to the specific needs of its customers.

The lean startup philosophy pushes web based or tech related startups away from the ideology of their dot-com era predecessors in order to achieve cost-effective production by building a minimal product and gauging customer feedback. We asserts that the "lean has nothing to do with how much money a company raises," rather it has everything to do with assessing the specific demands of consumers and how to meet that demand using the least amount of resources possible.

Chapter 15: Lean Startup Deployment

A minimum viable product (MVP) is the "version of a new product which allows a team to collect the maximum amount of validated learning about customers with the least effort." The goal of an MVP is to test fundamental business hypotheses (or leap-of-faith assumptions) and to help entrepreneurs begin the learning process as quickly as possible. As an example, Zappos founder Nick Swinmurn wanted to test the hypothesis that customers were ready and willing to buy shoes online. Instead of building a website and a large database of footwear, Swinmurn approached local shoe stores, took pictures of their inventory, posted the pictures online, bought the shoes from the stores at full price, and sold them directly to customers if they purchased the shoe through his website. Swinmurn deduced that customer demand was present, and Zappos would eventually grow into a billion dollar business based on the model of selling shoes online.

Continuous deployment

Continuous deployment is a process "whereby all code that is written for an application is immediately deployed into production," which results in a reduction of cycle times. Ries states that some of the companies he's worked with deploy new code into production as often as 50 times a day. The phrase was coined by Timothy Fitz, one of Ries's colleagues and an early engineer at IMVU.

Split testing

A split test or A/B test is an experiment in which "different versions of a product are offered to customers at the same time." The goal of a split test is to observe changes in behaviour between the two groups and to measure the impact of each version on an actionable metric.

A/B testing can also be performed in serial fashion where a group of users one week may see one version of the product while the next week users see another. This can be criticized in circumstances where external events may influence user behaviour one time period but not the other. For example a split test of two ice cream flavours performed in serial during the summer and winter would see a marked decrease in demand during the winter where that decrease is mostly related to the weather and not to the flavour offer.

Vanity metrics

Vanity metrics are measurements which give "the rosiest picture possible" but do not accurately reflect the key drivers of a business. This is in contrast to actionable metrics, the measurement of which can lead to a business decision and subsequent action.

Typical examples of a vanity metric are the number of new users gained per day. While a high number of users gained per day seems beneficial to any company, if the cost of acquiring each user through expensive advertising campaigns is significantly higher than the revenue gained per user, then gaining more users could quickly lead to bankruptcy.

Vanity metrics for one company may be actionable metrics for another. For example, a company specializing in creating web based dashboards for financial markets might view the number of web page views per person as a vanity metric as their revenue is not based on number of page views. However, an online magazine with advertising would view web page views as a key metric as page views as directly correlated to revenue.

Pivot

A pivot is a "structured course correction designed to test a new fundamental hypothesis about the product, strategy, and engine of growth." A notable example of a company employing the pivot is Groupon; when the company first started, it was an online activism platform called The Point. After receiving almost no traction, the founders opened a Wordpress blog and launched their first coupon promotion for a pizzeria located in their building lobby. Although they only received 20 redemptions, the founders realized that their idea was significant, and had successfully empowered people to coordinate group action. Three years later, Groupon would grow into a billion dollar business.

Chapter 16: Additional Lean Startup Concepts

The following represents a brief description of some of the main concepts associated with the Lean Startup approach.

1. **Test Frequently and Learn Quickly**

As the example in previous chapter of the MVP approach demonstrated, they advise that you don't build an elaborate product before you have undertaken numerous tests along the way (They are big advocates of A/B testing).

2. **Observe and Measure Real Customer Behaviour**

Avoid focus groups and watch how real customers behave. Getting the MVP into the hands of real customers early on and quickly learning from what they do underpins their entire methodology.

3. **Focus Exclusively on Capturing Actionable Metrics**

Avoid vanity metrics i.e. metrics that create a favourable impression about performance when they are illusory. For example: what good is one million page impressions if none of them convert? Instead entrepreneurs need to focus on actionable metrics i.e. real metrics which can inform decisions.

4. Be Comfortable Pivoting based on Key Learnings

We recommend you pivot or stop what you are doing if the initial plan is not working (and your findings support the view that changing direction is more likely to be successful than continuing with the original plan).

5. Embrace New Accounting Methods

Generally Accepted Accounting Principles (GAAP) has underpinned financial accounting for many years. However, we argue that Lean Startups need to embrace 'innovation accounting' before they get to the point where traditional accounting kicks in. With this method we suggests that progress is best tracked by observing things like user activity, engagement and retention. In other words, if user numbers are increasing, and they are being retained such that Life Time Value (LTV) is growing significantly, this is a better indicator of 'progress' than traditional accounting methods.

6. Stay Lean

The word 'lean' refers to speed and agility and not 'cost savings' as some readers misinterpret (although that said, they are against waste 'of all guises'). Again we are recommending that startups take advantage of the discovery mode to quickly learn what is not working so they can make changes immediately.

Chapter 17: Create Pre-Launch Demand

At one of the companies I use to work for, not only did we have Search Engine Optimisation (SEO) in place even before product development we also had a blog.

We talked about the problems we aimed to solve (the changing buyer-seller relationship) and which we knew our target audience faced and we mastered our strategy on approaching them.

Instead of beta testing a product, we beta tested an idea and integrated the feedback we received from our readers early on in our product development process. This strategy supports the Lean Startup approach. It means a lot to future customers to be in on the ground level and feel as though you are truly building a product specifically for them and the issues that keep them up at night.

By using this strategy, we began drumming up interest in our solutions with so much advance notice we had a pipeline of more than 16,000 interested buyers when the product came to market.

How does that compare to your last product release? Ask your salespeople. You say you don't have salespeople? Okay. Keep reading.

Spend to Sell

"Invest in your success" is corny but true and in this case, carries a couple different meanings. First off, forget about counting every last penny. Yes, the lean startup movement is correct in saying you shouldn't throw wild parties but isn't that just common sense? Where you should make serious spends is in areas that will eventually lead to sales down the road. And yes, naturally, that means investing in some quality salespeople, as well as quality sales and marketing tools to make it happen.

At the first instance you are able, start shifting funds from R&D into sales. As great as your product is, it won't sell itself, and you won't make any money unless you can actually make it move. As you look to expand your senior leadership team, make sure a Sales Director is one of your first hires.

But remember, sales cannot function to its true potential without marketing. Once you have salespeople in place, you need marketers and marketing tools to make sure they are in touch with the right people at the right time. Buyer-seller relationships are not what they used to be; buyers have far more access to information and make more judgments before engaging with sellers than ever before. That means it's marketing's responsibility to ultimately craft your public message, nurture leads, and monitor their sales readiness. With this in place your company can pursue the right leads and generate far more sales. Make sure your sales and marketing teams are in lockstep to drive revenue at a more efficient rate.

It's a terrible shame that so many entrepreneurs think sales and marketing teams can't be just as creative or innovative as product teams; don't be one of them. By bringing the right individuals on board, you enable your company to tell a dynamic story and bring far more context to the solutions your product offers that it might not tell on its own. It's a crowded world out there, and quality sales and marketing teams will help your company rise above the noise. That investment makes sure the best and boldest executives are accelerating product adoption and the revenue channel. And it lets your product team focus on their main initiatives; future product versions, and thinking about what things your thriving company might try next.

You can't be a startup forever. And you shouldn't want to. The lean startup model only offers tools to get you so far. By implementing these tips into your growing business, you'll be better poised for long-term success down the road, wherever your company chooses to roam. Trade the lean for the green. Revenue and growth are great, great things.

Chapter 18: Deploy Decision like a Lean Startup

Successful companies thrive on their ability to make good decisions, quickly. Unfortunately, most business intelligence projects move slowly. Several lean startup principles can help you reverse the status-quo, set new performance levels, and be a change-agent. The cornerstone of working lean is to learn and apply the learning as fast as possible. Sounds simple enough, here is what you do:

1. Test a hypothesis.
2. Build a minimum viable product (prototype).
3. Release in small batches.

However, business intelligence organizations are structured exactly OPPOSITE of the lean model:

1. Define every requirement up front.
2. Build without collecting feedback.
3. Only deliver "complete" solutions.

Picture your team as a startup company that wants customers using (and buying) their product ASAP. The business intelligence community must work with the exact same mind-set to help their companies gain a competitive edge.

Test a Hypothesis

Always begin by clearly understanding the decision your "customer" wants to make. A business intelligence premise is that if you give someone the right information, they can/will be able to take action. How often do reports go unused or not acted upon in your organization? Doesn't that frustrate you? Therefore, you must test the following hypothesis at each step of your project to ensure your work is directly tied into the needs of the organization. Customers will take action on the decision, given the appropriate data in a usable form.

Address one decision at a time; you don't need an exhaustive list to get started. When you ask someone what decision they are trying to make, they typically will respond with wanting to know about data. To flush out the decision, here is the type of discussion you should lead.

You: What decision are you trying to make?

Customer: What were our sales in each region last month?

You: If you knew that information, what would you do?

Customer: I could tell each salesperson if they need to sell more.

You: How would you decide if they are selling enough?

Customer: Well, first I would need to compare sales to targets.

You: That makes sense. How far off target gets you concerned?

Customer: More than 5% behind could be a problem.

You: What else do you need?

Customer: If they trended down the last three months.

You: So, is the decision: "Do I need to work with the salesperson to increase sales of specific products?"

Customer: Yes, I agree. This was really helpful!

Once you know the decision, it is helpful to frame the supporting data as a results statement and validate it with your customer; the salesperson must be at least 5% behind target and trending down the last three months. Is that correct?" The simple results statement is incredibly powerful. If the criteria are not met, they do not need to think about taking further action. All the noise from irrelevant data is cleared away. I AM NOT saying someone can make a final decision with this information alone; rather, it indicates an action may be necessary. Also, someone will likely conduct a more detailed analysis based on the observed results.

Build a Minimum Viable Product Prototype

The decision and results statements are initial requirements for your visualization and building a minimum viable product (MVP). The MVP is the simplest means to collect feedback from customers and refine until your customer agrees with the hypothesis: "They will take action on the decision, given the appropriate data in a usable form." By "minimum," the MVP is not about trying to deliver a final product (visualization) with a limited number of features; although, you would not want to deliver more than needed. If you were truly a startup, the MVP would test the viability of your business idea.

You don't need design software to build the prototype. Let me say it another way; don't use design software. Head up to a whiteboard with a black marker. Most clients I work with initially think this rudimentary approach is not worthwhile. The basis of working lean is to move quickly, and they soon realize that choosing colours or making detailed designs is distracting and time consuming (you will find it hard to write any level of detail with a thick marker).

Within 30 minutes, put your energy into volume and variation of ideas. It's only important to rough out the visualizations, continue the discussion, and get feedback. Ask everyone for his or her initial reactions and interpretations; first-impressions are key. For example, this sketch might start a conversation around what decision is needed if the salesperson is above target but trending down for three months (i.e., Product); that should turn out to be more critical that the original decision you are testing!

Decision: "Do I need to work with the salesperson to increase sales of specific products?"

Results Statement: "The salesperson must be at least 5% behind target and trending down the last three months."

There are phone apps to snap pictures of the whiteboard and stitch the images together. If you work on paper, stick with one idea per page so you can swap sections to create the best story without having to redraft all other elements. Your finished product may, of course, combine ideas onto a single dashboard/screen.

In whatever form you capture the prototype, you will need to make a final version, clean and legible, along with notes explaining interactions, legends, etc. You can just make neater drawings or use computer software (PowerPoint, KeyNote, Visio, etc). You might find that recording concepts and operating intent is enough; the detailed requirements will be determined during development as the team works collaboratively. Keep thinking and acting lean.

Release in Small Batches

The practice of delivering a "complete" set of visualization solutions just doesn't work; it never really did. For a long time, people have felt secure using this approach. However, if it takes a few months, or even one month, to write "all" the requirements and then develop, there is a good chance the requirements will have changed. All the while, your customers wait helplessly without any visualizations. Can you see how delivering more frequent, smaller releases creates opportunities to move the business forward by making decisions sooner? Doesn't it make sense to receive and incorporate feedback from real-world use before building out too far?

Everyone involved with the business intelligence solution, most importantly your customer, must agree to work in this model or it doesn't work. People will be a bit unnerved because they are comfortable in the current long-cycle model; they know (or think they know) how the project is going to turn out. Shifting to a small-release model will initially generate feelings of uncertainty and doubt. It seems ad hoc when in fact there is a solid process. After a few releases, people will begin to see the impact. You have to help the organization cope with withdrawal as they rid themselves of old dependencies. You can ease the transition by encouraging collaboration and reinforcing the benefits of small batches over detailed requirements and complete solutions.

1. Keep a list of all decisions/results hypotheses that have been tested or need to be tested.
2. Meet once a week to review and reprioritize the list.
3. Be okay with stopping work and switching to something that becomes more important.
4. Fix what's broken right away.
5. Test hypotheses in parallel with developing finished releases.
6. Create rough deadlines for each release; it's helpful to have a target.
7. Make everyone responsible for QA. Don't put it all on development's shoulders.

8. Treat enhancements as a new prototype to test; don't just add them in.

Chapter 19: Think Big, Start Small

Small startup companies have an advantage; they can test innovative ideas quickly.

Some of our best ideas supposedly come to us in the shower, on the road when we are driving or for me in kitchen when I am cooking. I always think of a business to start, an industry to shake up. Or maybe not!

When we are in the shower, when we are thinking about our idea; boy, does it sound brilliant. But the reality is that most of our ideas are actually terrible, but it's hard to know which are the brilliant ones, and which are the crazy ones, until we actually test them against reality.

The Lean Startup, about innovation in an evolving marketplace; it is okay to put a totally unfinished product out onto the market, sometimes it is actually better.

It is a really paradoxical thing that we want to think big, but start small. And then scale fast. As an example, Facebook has gone from obscurity to ubiquity in less than a decade.

We have a tendency to see the world the way it is, and to think it will always be that way, Facebook actually faced very stiff competition from the now-forgotten market leaders at that time however Facebook had the best growth model, one which allowed the company to surpass its rivals very quickly.

It is easier to innovate at small companies that lack the rigorous planning of a large corporation, and that is true not just for startups in the tech world, but for entrepreneurs who have a great idea for a new product.

These days, young companies don't even have to build a factory to create their products; they can just take part in what is call outsourcing of the means of production.

Even if you want to build a physical device, you can just build a computer schematic of what you want, and there are manufacturers now who will send you a batch of, say, 40 of those, at a very low cost. That process can allow young companies to compete with large, established corporations.

The truth is, we actually have more stuff than we know what to do with, so, building more of it, more efficiently, actually doesn't help. We have to be focused on the efficiency with which we can test new ideas to discover which are brilliant, and which are crazy.

Chapter 20: The Promise of the Lean Startup

Today's high-tech entrepreneurs have at their command more than just the ability to invent in new technologies. They have mastered the discipline and methodology required to harness those technologies in order to serve customers. Such a combination of new technology and new understanding is unlocking new opportunities. In order to maximize them, this generation of entrepreneurs combines extremely low costs with faster cycle times to produce what I call "lean startups."

Total startup costs are plummeting: It costs less than £5,000 to launch a new, web-based product. Using the latest technology, a lean startup can create product prototypes in weeks and months instead of years, using customer feedback to evolve them in near-real time. Releases are measured in minutes and hours, not days and weeks. In some cases, lean startups are releasing new code to production 50 times a day.

Parallel to the work by the "solution team" (engineering, operations and quality assurance), there is a new kind of "problem team" what we used to call business development, marketing, and sales; that is asking such bigger questions as. Who will our customers be?

What problem does our product solve for them?

How many of them are there?

How will we reach them?

A lean startup is built to learn

The problem team is not merely engaged in a series of whiteboard exercises. They are working to validate or refute their hypotheses and then to share their findings with the rest of the company so they can be used to reduce uncertainty and further chart the enterprise's future. Each iteration leads to a "pivot" in which the company systematically changes some part of its vision to adapt to reality.

The ultimate goal of a lean startup is to identify where its vision intersects with what reality can accommodate. It is neither a capitulation to "what customers think they want" nor a wilful ignorance of conditions on the ground. It is a company built to learn.

As a consequence, this new startup is relentlessly metrics-driven. It tries out new ideas with a fraction of customers in order to make a priority of using facts, not opinions. Its unit of progress is that of validated learning about its customers. Because this radical notion of progress is located firmly in the heads of its employees, and not in any artefacts they produce, the lean startup is employee-centric and knowledge-obsessed. It is a truly fun place to work.

Rational, vital entrepreneurship

The lean startup gets faster and more agile over time, even as it scales. Instead of seeing process as a synonym for bureaucracy, it sees it as a synonym for discipline. Focusing all of its energy on only those activities that matter, it frees up time and energy for true productivity. It represents, in other words, a transformation every bit as significant as the advent of lean manufacturing.

Just-in-time inventory control, an end to time-quality-money, "pick two" thinking, and true continuous improvement are at the heart of the supply chains that feed, clothe, and sustain the developed world. They were made possible by a combination of new technologies and new thinking. The lean startup heralds a similar promise: that the practice of entrepreneurship can be put on solid, rigorous, footing.

Considering the incredible amount of human energy, passion, and creativity that we currently invest in creating new products and services, it's a terrible waste that so many of them fail. The promise of the lean startup is that instead of building our companies according to myths, we can guide them with facts and the knowledge required to use those facts well. Put another way, we won't waste our time building products or services that nobody wants.

The lean startup model eliminates waste and focuses on customer feedback to build a product or provide a service that people want. The model requires business owners to focus more on knowing who their customers are and understanding how they will attract and maintain them.

Given the success of small business owners who have used this model to grow their businesses quickly, it's become a popular model for budding business owners. However, there are still challenges entrepreneurs should be aware of when following the lean startup model. A few suggestions on how to handle them follow.

Be flexible

This is critical when dealing with customers and building your project or service on the fly. Be prepared for customers to change their minds, miss deadlines, and have high expectations. It may seem like a pain but in the long run it will be well worth it when your product or service is customized to solve a customer's problems.

Talk to your customers

Find out what they want and don't want. Build your product or design your service to accommodate their needs. Allow them to have input on and validate your pricing. Never build a final product and then ask if the customer wants it.

Develop a social media strategy

Determine which social media outlet will benefit your company most. For example, if your company is a consumer company, Facebook may work better for you and more effectively get you in front of your target audience.

Use a customer relationship tool

This will allow you to keep your customers. It is a critical component. If you don't know how to do this, you'll be a one-hit wonder.

In my experience, the lean startup model requires discipline and focus to adhere to the customer feedback that is so essential to achieving success. When a business owner uses it properly, he or she can avoid a lot of the pain commonly associated with starting a business.

Chapter 21: A Lean Startup Doesn't Necessarily Mean Small

Strategic marketing is a fundamental aspect of the lean startup methodology. And lean startup itself as a process for bringing technology to market warrants careful consideration by any entrepreneur in the socially enabled age of Web.

Lean can be define in the sense of low burn. Of course, many startups are capital efficient and generally frugal. But by taking advantage of open source, agile software, and iterative development, lean startups can operate with much less waste.

Lean startup as an application of lean thinking, which at its most basic is about maximizing the value you provide to your customers while minimizing waste in your organization. If it ain't focused on delivering value to the customer, get rid of it.

Lean startup is powered by these drivers:
1. The use of platforms enabled by open source and free software.
2. The application of agile development methodologies, which dramatically reduce waste and unlock creativity in product development.

My belief is that these lean startups will achieve dramatically lower development costs, faster time to market, and higher quality products in the years to come, whether they also lead to dramatically higher returns for investors is a question I am looking forward to studying.

Now, there is obviously a bias here in favour of software plays and web startups, but the spirit behind lean startup and its roots in the broader lean thinking philosophy means there are powerful lessons to be learned here too for hardware plays that have to manufacture and ship a physical product. The whole lean movement, after all, had its origins on the Toyota assembly line decades ago.

Lean has nothing to do with small; in fact the amount of capital you take in has nothing to do with whether or not your ambitions are big or small. I have seen some of the confusion in the market where the TechCrunch people are talking about the battle between the super angels and the VCs and I fundamentally believe that this just reflects the confusion in that marketplace.

For example Microsoft and Apple as tech titans that got to market with only a couple of million dollars. "Even eBay, the amount that they raised, they never used.

So the best companies end up being extremely capital efficient ... lean is not small, Lean is a tactic by which we help our entrepreneurs and our entrepreneurs help themselves in a data-driven way figure out how they are going to iterate their product. And through data and through vision, we also pivot that business model if we believe the business model no longer works.

The best entrepreneurs incorporate lean techniques but are driven by the big vision, Bill Gates, Steve Jobs, Larry Ellison, and all other successful entrepreneurs had a clear vision in mind, and that is the story we all know well. What we did not see was the journey and the many steps (and missteps) that they took along the way in reaching that vision. There were pivots and dives and tucks and all sorts of contortions to get where they sit today.

I would advises startups to instead focus on what type of problem they are trying to solve, rather than on whether their idea is big enough.

Are you tackling a broad and incredibly complex problem where there is no precedent or are you tackling a specific problem that has some proof points and validation of a recognizable problem? Once you know the type of problem you are tackling, then you can better assess your journey and the tools to use in guiding your way, whether it is lean startup or some other approach.

Chapter 22: Top 10 Ways Entrepreneurs Pivot a Lean Startup

The popular view of a real entrepreneur is someone with a big vision, and a stubborn determination to charge straight ahead through any obstacle and make it happen. The vision part is fine, but successful entrepreneurs have found that the extreme uncertainty of a new product or service usually requires many course corrections, or "pivots" to find a successful formula.

This reality has fostered a popular new startup approach which dramatically improves the efficiency and speed of these corrections. Today's entrepreneurs use continuous innovation to create radically successful businesses.

Eric espouses designing products with the smallest set of features to please a customer base, and moving products into the marketplace quickly to test reaction, then iterating. He does a great job in the book of making the case for management systems, rather than gut-level reactions, to make required course corrections (pivots), to dramatically improve the odds for success.

Pivots come in many different flavours, each designed to test the viability of a different hypothesis about the product, business model, and engine of growth. I agree with Eric's summary of the top ten types of pivots to consider:

1. Zoom-in pivot. In this case, what previously was considered a single feature in a product becomes the whole product. This highlights the value of "focus" and "minimum viable product" (MVP), delivered quickly and efficiently.

2. Zoom-out pivot. In the reverse situation, sometimes a single feature is insufficient to support a customer set. In this type of pivot, what was considered the whole product becomes a single feature of a much larger product.

3. Customer segment pivot. Your product may attract real customers, but not the ones in the original vision. In other words, it solves a real problem, but needs to be positioned for a more appreciative segment, and optimized for that segment.

4. Customer need pivot. Early customer feedback indicates that the problem solved is not very important, or money isn't available to buy. This requires repositioning, or a completely new product, to find a problem worth solving.

5. Platform pivot. This refers to a change from an application to a platform, or vice versa. Many founders envision their solution as a

platform for future products, but don't have a single killer application just yet. Most customers buy solutions, not platforms.

6. Business architecture pivot. Geoffrey Moore, many years ago, observed that there are two major business architectures: high margin, low volume (complex systems model), or low margin, high volume (volume operations model). You can't do both at the same time.

7. Value capture pivot. This refers to the monetization or revenue model. Changes to the way a startup captures value can have far-reaching consequences for business, product, and marketing strategies. The "free" model doesn't capture much value.

8. Engine of growth pivot. Most startups these days use one of three primary growth engines: the viral, sticky, and paid growth models. Picking the right model can dramatically affect the speed and profitability of growth.

9. Channel pivot. In sales terminology, the mechanism by which a company delivers it product to customers is called the sales channel or distribution channel. Channel pivots usually require unique pricing, feature, and competitive positioning adjustments.

10. Technology pivot. Sometimes a startup discovers a way to achieve the same solution by using a completely different technology.

This is most relevant if the new technology can provide superior price and/or performance to improve competitive posture.

Every entrepreneur faces the challenge in developing a product of deciding when to pivot and when to persevere. Ask most entrepreneurs who have decided to pivot and they will tell you that they wish they had made the decision sooner. In fact, a startup's runway is really not money, but the number of pivots they can still make. What are you doing to get to the required pivots faster?

Always, think about your exit strategy

While it is great to be thinking about growing a business, one should always be working on an exit strategy. You should consider what would make you move away from the business. If so what would you do next? It is true that strategic entrepreneurs always keep their options open and manage their business well so that the business is always in sales-worthy shape.

No one knows what opportunities the future will bring, but with these tips and helpful guidelines, you can be sure that you are now fully equipped to step out and make those opportunities work for you.

Chapter 23: Some Criticism of Lean Startup

Much of what has been written and said about lean startups makes good sense. However, that advice is often incomplete, and some of the things left unsaid are the least intuitive...There are only two priorities for a startup: Winning the market and not running out of cash. Running lean is not an end. For that matter, neither is running fat. Both are tactics that you use to win the market and not run out of cash before you do so. By making "running lean" an end, you may lose your opportunity to win the market, either because you fail to fund the R&D necessary to find product/market fit or you let a competitor out-execute you in taking the market. Sometimes running fat is the right thing to do.

For me, I feel that regardless of the concept, people will always find flaws and have strong counter arguments to certain elements of the approach. Awareness of these arguments helps entrepreneurs make more informed decisions regarding whether or not they embrace alternative approaches. They are merely opinions after all.

If you are an Internet or technology based startup the lessons will be ones that are likely to resonate. The Lean Startup approach is certainly one which will help you instil early on the need for decisions to be based on scientific facts (as much as possible) and that given the extremely difficult conditions start-ups operate in, that an ability to learn quickly and change tack are lessons you would do well to bear in mind. I for one have been converted to their way of thinking.

Last year, from Silicon Valley to Wall Street, it was impossible to escape the concept of the "Lean Startup" especially the great ideas espoused by the preeminent thought leader on the topic, Eric Ries.

Hundreds, if not thousands, of entrepreneurs embraced these tenets and joined the "Lean Startup movement." In addition to curbing costs, an entrepreneur would begin by creating their first "minimal viable product" to test that initial business idea. If it failed? No big deal! The strategy of launching quietly held that few people would even know about the product in the first place and thus wouldn't have been the wiser to its initial failure. Eventually, the goal was to achieve product/market fit another Riesian commandment that equates to ploughing through "build-measure-learn" feedback loops until one discovers that special (and monetizable) moment when a product and its market interest collide.

But there are also tremendous drawbacks and limits to the Lean Startup cycle of listen/respond/fail/adapt. In life and in business, failure can mean certain death, without a chance for another loop. Indeed, too many startups have died (or are doomed to) by applying this method to their businesses, especially as their investors watch in horror.

Don't be in a rush to get big," Ries once said, "be in a rush to have a great product."

I am here to tell you that it's not either/or. You can be in a rush to be both big and to have a great product. After all, you only get one shot to make a real splash with a product launch and truly impress the world, right? I don't believe in the strategy of rushing a product to market as cheaply as possible and hoping for the best. Yes, there are plenty of entrepreneurs who swear it works and have the good fortune to be able to prove that. But there are a lot more who don't. It can also seriously hinder growth and limit revenue potential. And when you are a startup founder, shouldn't you (and your investors) be all about growing your company, delighting your customers, and bringing in the big bucks?

With the right manoeuvres, a company can best use its money to both grow fast and grow smart. Unlike the Lean Startup methods, this enables measurable and repeatable success.

Here are a few proven ways to launch big, not lean:

Build the Route to Market in Parallel to Building Your Product

Many great products have failed because there were no buyers or users ready. Remember Pets.com? Of course you do but for entirely the wrong reasons. It is vital to remember that building a viable sales channel is just as important as building the viable product itself.

The Lean Startup method would have you rush a product to market. Then, you would maybe flounder on initial launch but iterate nonstop and put what few, loyal customers adopt early through countless revisions, updates, and interface changes. Finally, you might eke out a product worth the mass market's purchasing dollars.

But what happens if your product development issues are so vast that it leads to poor word-of-mouth? What happens if you have no other leads in the pipeline ready for your robust, top-of-class final product? Well, then you have put in all that effort for zero payoff. It is terrible to push for so long on a bootstrapped budget and then be stuck saying, "Now what?"

Chapter 24: Managing Change and Growth in Startup

Inside tips on how managers can deal with staffing challenges in a growing startup with Biotech Company as a model example.

Like all businesses, life science companies face the trying challenges of accessing sufficient capital, wisely allocating constrained resources, developing and executing beneficially designed collaborations and partnerships, demonstrating the courage to make difficult, sometimes complex, go/no-go decisions, making appropriate risk assessment and effectively managing assets. Today, with over 100 biotech products on the market and sales of the top 24 such products reaching $1 billion in 2006, the dynamic changes that life science companies experience on the way to product success are, at once, essential and unnerving. Priorities change; goals and objectives are revised often; new skills and talent are required in the transition from discovery research to product development and beyond; some existing roles and responsibilities narrow, others broaden; infrastructure strengthens; and resources are regularly reallocated.

Commonly in startup companies, a research project or program that may have initially been highly valued by investors and exciting to company founders is surpassed by another project that may appear closer to moving into clinical studies. In such cases projects may be dropped or their resources diverted elsewhere.

Researchers are known to work many extra hours to advance 'skunk works' projects that they believe in and find exciting, yet that are not sufficiently resourced by the company. Overall, resources once liberally provided for discovery research are often redirected to fund process and product development, clinical studies, regulatory affairs and manufacturing. The effective integration of new, different skill sets as a product moves into the clinic, clears regulatory hurdles and readies for commercial launch is a complex challenge. Such major changes significantly affect employees both professionally and emotionally.

Most people respond to change by passing though four phases. First, they deny that the change is occurring. Next, most resist accepting the change, while slowly but surely gathering more information about what the change means. At this point, they are in a position to begin to consider alternatives and possibilities. Finally, they arrive at a readiness to accept the change and start making it work for them. People move through change with varying degrees of comfort and at their own unique paces. Wise leaders consider the impact of change on employees, increase communication at such times and provide sufficient focus for meaningful work to continue with minimized distress and distraction.

Growth and staffing

As biotech companies move beyond discovery research through drug development, different skills and talent become necessary. New functions emerge. Cross-functional project teams form. Some temporary employees, advisors and consultants may be replaced by full-time staff. Hint: Find ways to communicate with existing staff about the skills and outcomes that the new functions bring.

Hiring may accelerate. The pressures of adding staff to meet the demands of growth makes it tempting to 'squint' at the qualifications of candidates in the hope of seeing what we would like to see. Hint: Hold out for the right skills in the right person. Mismatches in skills or other success factors often result in time-consuming setbacks.

The proliferation of new functions and activities and the expanding head count usually trigger expanded infrastructure. It is very challenging to develop infrastructure that is sufficiently lean yet adequate to support activities across a company. Too little support can limit progress, and too much infrastructure can impede decision-making and interfere with the agility essential to growth. Hint: Keep infrastructure, systems and processes simple, lean and optimally productive.

Some employees, often founding employees, who thrive during the startup phase, may struggle to settle into satisfying and meaningful roles in the changing company. Hint: Be creative in designing roles that both meet company needs and play to the strengths of the individual. Where an appropriate match cannot be found, be thoughtful and considerate in determining how founding employees can be treated respectfully and fairly in such changing times.

Retaining key contributors in changing times

To ensure employee retention during periods of change, compensation (base pay, bonuses and stock options) should be strongly competitive. Care should be taken to value key people, in terms of their criticality, productivity and versatility. The critical contributors are those considered 'show stoppers' individuals whose departure would adversely impact the company's success. Productive contributors, although perhaps not valued quite as highly as 'show stoppers,' would be very difficult to replace, as significant lost time would result. And versatile contributors, though not in either of these categories, have unique skill combinations that are especially critical to the organization. It pays to ensure that these key contributors are appropriately compensated and that they know how highly the company values their contribution.

Communicating change

In the absence of clear communication about exactly what is changing, why it is changing and what it means to individuals and teams, employees' imaginations can run wild, and usually not in positive directions. People tend to assume the worst, speculate and try to predict what is to come. Often, employees feel that information is being withheld from them, when it is more likely that the specifics of the changes are not yet clear enough to be communicated.

Invest time and effort to anticipate the questions and concerns of those affected by changes. Effectively communicating the 'what,' 'why' and 'how' of the changes directly affects the degree and duration of the distractions that come with change.

Change is challenging. Uncertainty is highly distracting. Leaders who consciously consider the questions, concerns and anxieties of individuals and teams and who communicate clearly and effectively while implementing changes can expect strong cooperation and good results. Employees who hold reasonable expectations of their leaders during times of change and who work to understand the changes and the possibilities for the future can be ready to make the most of their next steps.

The road from promises to products is smoother and more fulfilling for life science companies that are willing to pay competitively, communicate clearly and often, address questions and conflicts directly and in a timely way, resist over-building or under-building infrastructure, and actively manage employee expectations.

Chapter 25: Conclusion

If you are thinking about creating a startup, do your homework and learn about lean startup. Don't spend six months coding a product; prove that people want to buy it first.

Have you ever thought about creating your own software startup? Perhaps you're a great programmer with an idea for the next Twitter or Facebook. Maybe you have an itch you need to scratch. Or maybe you just want to learn what it feels like to be an entrepreneur.

Go for it! This is a great time to build a startup, and there is no substitute for just doing it.

Developers usually resist lean startup; when you have a great idea, you want to open Visual Studio and build it! You probably figure you will worry about all that sales and business stuff after you have perfected your software. It doesn't usually work. Lean startup flips these activities around, and it takes some getting used to, just as it takes practice to get used to agile concepts like writing tests first and pair programming. Now you are not just building software, you are building a business.

To move your business forward, you have to learn. Just as agile prescribes building the "simplest thing that could possibly work," lean startup prescribes building the "minimum viable product" or MVP. You have to constantly ask yourself, "What is the absolute least I can build to test my next business hypothesis?" If you prove your hypothesis, go further in that direction. If you disprove it, you pivot into a new direction. Just as with agile iterations, early cycles of build-measure-learn should probably take a week or two, not six months.

These principles apply whether you are a one-person bootstrapper or a VC-funded hotshot. There is simply no reason to build something until you have proven that people will buy it and that customers will pay more than it costs to acquire them. Even though you are probably more comfortable programming, get the selling right first. I can't stress this enough: spend your upfront energy proving that you can make money, instead of writing code.

Just as agile strives for tight iterations for software development; lean startup strives for a tight cycle of build-measure-learn. Instead of spending six months building something that you hope customers will buy, lean startup suggests building the smallest thing that you can measure effectively to learn if you are moving your business forward or if you need to "pivot" in a different direction.

The most important business question is whether or not people will buy your product; so instead of building it, make a webpage with a "click here to buy" button and see if you can get people to click on it. If people click the button, then you ask for their email address to let them know when the product will be ready. If nobody clicks on it, then are you not happy that you did not build the product?

Think about that for a second. That Big Idea of yours; how long would it take you to build it? Six months? A year? More? Have you proven that people will pay for it once you build it? How long would it take you to build a simple webpage describing your product, selling your product with a "click here to buy" button? A day or two? If you can't sell it, why build it?

What are the consequences of spending six months or a year building something only to find out people don't actually want it (or don't want to pay for it)? For most people, it would be devastating. It would drain your finances and bruise your ego. By contrast, what are the consequences of finding out that nobody clicks on your landing page? Not much; it simply means you have to try again with another idea; you need to pivot and because you only spent a day or two attempting to validate this idea, you probably still have the energy and resources to pivot toward another one.

Even when you build a simple Web page to validate your idea, you still have to figure out how to get people to visit it. Unless you are already a celebrity or have thousands of Twitter followers, that likely means "renting" traffic by paying for Google or Bing search terms.

Every commerce site has a "conversion rate": for every 100 visitors, let's say only one will buy; that's a 1 percent conversion rate. If you have an idea of your conversion rate (perhaps from people clicking on your Buy button) and you know how much it costs to generate 100 visitors (from paying Google or Bing), then you know how much you need to make from each customer who buys. If you test a 1 percent conversion rate for a $25 product, and it only costs $15-20 to get 100 visitors, that's a good sign you can profit.

On the other hand, if the cost of acquiring customers is greater than what you can charge those customers, then you will fail, no matter how great your idea seems. In practice, online businesses that would likely be found using very common or general search terms are incredibly difficult to pull off, because those search terms are expensive.

There is no reason to guess; you can prove whether or not people will pay a profitable price for your product before you even build it by creating a landing page and paying to drive traffic to it. If you can charge more than it costs to drive traffic, you have a winner. If not, it's time to pivot. That's lean startup in a nutshell.

Good Luck!

Resource and References

Shigeo Shingo; Fundamental Principles of Lean Manufacturing

Shigeo Shingo; Non-Stock Production: The Shingo System of Continuous Improvement

Shigeo Shingo; A Study of the Toyota Production System from an Industrial Engineering Viewpoint

Drucker, P., "What Makes an Effective Executive", Harvard Business review, June 2004

Lessons from Toyota's long drive, an interview with Katsuaki Watanabe, HBR, July 2007

Liker, J. & D. Meier, Toyota Talent, McGraw Hill, 2007

Shook, J. , Managing To Learn, Lean Enterprise Institute 2008

Fishman, C., "No Satisfaction", Fast Company, Dec 2006/Jan 2007

The Lean Startup: How Today's Entrepreneurs Use Continuous Innovation to Create Radically Successful Businesses by Eric Ries (Sep 13, 2011)